FOOD AND FARMING

Written by
Andrew Charman

Illustrated by
Andrew Wheatcroft, Roger Stewart,
Rachel Ross and Mike Atkinson

Edited by
Lyn Saville and Alison Cooper

Designed by
Clare Davey

Picture Research by
Helen Taylor

CONTENTS

The food we eat

Nearly all the food we eat comes from farmers: eggs from chickens, meat and milk from animals, or plants such as wheat, potatoes and apples. Other products such as wool, cotton and rubber are also produced by farmers whose land is kept just for that purpose. This is what farming means: using land to grow crops and rear animals to provide food and other products for people.

People have farmed for thousands of years in nearly every part of the world. If you could go back in time, you would find that all our ancestors were farmers. Today, we don't all have to work on farms. This is because many farmers are able to produce extra food which they can sell to us. But this is not the case worldwide, as many farmers are struggling to produce enough food to feed themselves and their families.

The meals we eat are made up of many different ingredients. Each kind of food gives our bodies different nutrients that we need to stay healthy. Today, these foods rarely come from one farm. Even a simple meal may contain foods that were grown thousands of miles apart.

In developed countries supermarkets sell food from all over the world. In developing countries people go to markets to buy locally grown food.

3

Key words

Developing countries - poor countries in the process of improving farming, making better roads, providing more efficient production techniques and improving people's life chances.

Developed countries - rich countries with access to health care, education, political and social security, and with a higher standard of living.

Pineapple - grown on the Ivory Coast, Africa

Carrots - grown in England

Burgers - made from beef raised in the USA

Bananas - from Colombia, South America

Milk - from England

Juice - made from oranges grown in Spain

Peas - grown in England

Ketchup - made from tomatoes

Grapes - grown in Israel

Bread - made from wheat grown in Canada

Apples - from France

The farmer's work

There are farms all over the world and they are often very different from each other. They have different kinds of weather, soil, animals and crops, but wherever a farm is, there are some jobs that all farmers must do. *When* the farmer does them will depend on the seasons and the growing cycles of his crops and animals.

Growing crops

The ground must be prepared before the seed can be sown. Plant food, such as manure, is often added, then the ground is ploughed. The ploughing breaks up the surface and buries the plant food. The seed can then be sown.

The growing crops must be protected from weeds, disease and pests. They must also have light and water. In dry countries, farmers spend much of their time getting water to their crops.

When the crop has grown, it must be gathered in, or harvested. This is often the farmer's busiest time. In countries such as Britain, where the weather is cold in winter and warm in summer, the harvest usually takes place before the winter comes. In tropical countries, where it is warm all year round, the harvest can take place at any time of the year. The farmer can spread his workload by growing crops which become ready for harvesting at different times of the year.

These Thai farmers are harvesting Chinese cabbages. Their supply of food or money for the year to come will depend on a good harvest.

This farmer in Mali, Africa, is sowing seed by hand. In other parts of the world farmers use machines to do this.

On both high-tech and much simpler farms, the animals must be fed daily. In the US farm above, the cattle feed is delivered by truck. The African girl is feeding a calf by hand.

Keeping animals

Many farms keep animals as well as crops. Some farms keep only animals. Farm animals need constant care. Providing the animals with food and water is a daily task. Cleaning them out and checking their health also has to be carried out frequently. Animals are mated at certain times of the year and when the young are being born the farmer can be working round the clock.

In some parts of the world, farming has changed a great deal over the centuries. Jobs such as ploughing, planting, harvesting, milking and feeding, that were once done by hand, are now carried out by people using huge machines. In other parts of the world farming methods have hardly changed at all, and the majority of the work is still done by hand. In spite of the differences, these two kinds of farming still have much in common.

The origins of farming

People have not always farmed. Thousands of years ago, people lived by gathering nuts, berries and fruits, and by catching fish and hunting wild animals. Today, there are people living in rain forests who still get their food in this way. It is not an easy lifestyle. There is always a danger that there will not be enough food. Perhaps that is why people first started farming.

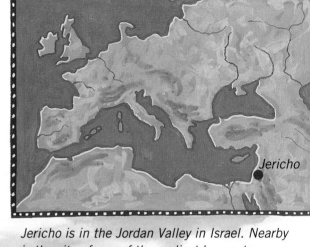

Jericho is in the Jordan Valley in Israel. Nearby is the site of one of the earliest known towns.

Before farming began, people hunted animals and gathered nuts, roots, leaves and fruits for food.

Settling down to farm

The first farming probably involved keeping animals. Instead of hunting, people gathered wild sheep and goats into herds. These herds had to be moved from place to place to find fresh grazing. In East Africa there are still people living this way. Real farming began when people settled in one place and grew crops.

At first, most farmers grew just enough food to feed themselves. If they were very skilful, or had particularly fertile land, they could grow more than they needed. This surplus food could be exchanged for other products, or paid as a tax. Taxes would go to support priests, governments and armies.

An early farmer from Jericho, about 8000 years ago. He is harvesting wheat with a stone sickle fixed to a bone handle.

Key words
Fertile land - land with good soil producing lots of vegetation or crops.

Oasis - a fertile spot in a desert, where water is found.

The beginnings of civilization

A surplus of crops means that other people can make a living doing something other than farming. The earliest evidence we have of farming comes from Jericho in the Middle East.

The Jericho farmers of 7000 BC were successful because they had plenty of water to make crops grow. Gallons of water still pour out of the city's spring every day, turning that part of the desert into a green oasis.

Changing the crop

Emmer and einkorn are species of wild wheat. The ears of wild wheat are small and shatter easily. This means that the grain is easily loosened and lost on the ground. In order to be able to resow the grain, the first farmers selected it from the biggest and toughest ears. Eventually, farmers crossed wild emmer with a weedy grass to get bread wheat. The grains of this wheat are not lost easily. They have to be loosened by being beaten or threshed. They are then ground to make flour which is used to make bread.

Emmer

Einkorn

Bread wheat

Ancient farming

All living creatures need water. The first farmers lived in dry parts of the world - in Egypt, Iraq and India. In these countries there were rivers which overflowed every year. The farmers found ways of getting water to more of the land. This is called irrigation.

Farming in ancient Egypt

In Egypt the land is very hot and dry. The ancient Egyptians of 3000 BC were able to farm and flourish, because their great river, the Nile, flooded every year. A wide strip of land was covered with water for three months. When the river shrank back, it left behind a thin layer of rich, dark silt, ideal for growing crops. The farmers turned the soil with a light, wooden plough called an ard.

Some of the Nile's water was collected in broad, shallow troughs called 'basins'. It was then allowed to flood a field for about forty days before being drained back into the river. The land was then ploughed. This form of irrigation was used for centuries.

Later, water was transported to fields by a series of canals. The water in the canals was taken from a well, or the river, using a shaduf. With this method the fields could be given water whenever they needed it.

Egypt Extra
• The ancient Egyptians believed that they could carry on farming in the life after death.
• The Egyptians invented calendars so that they would know when to plant and harvest their crops.

The ancient Egyptians used a water-lifting device called a shaduf. Water could be transferred from a river or a well to canals running to the fields.

Like the ancient Egyptians, the Chinese rice growers were experts at irrigation. Here, foot-power is being used to raise water into the paddy-fields.

Rice farming in China

From 960-1279 the River Yangtze in China became the centre of a boom in rice farming. The paddy-fields were flooded with water from the river. It was kept in place by raised banks. Water buffalo pulled the ploughs and the rice seedlings were planted by hand by families working as teams.

At harvest time, the fields were drained and the rice cut with hand-held sickles. Quick-growing types of rice meant that two or three crops could be grown every year. Ducks, fish and water chestnuts provided food and were kept in the flooded channels between the fields.

The first farming tools

Early farming tools were made mostly of wood, bone and stone.

1. The digging stick was weighted with a stone to help it dig into the soil.

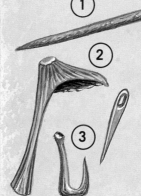

2. A sickle was used to cut crops such as wheat and barley. It was made of sharp flint, sometimes wedged into a handle of bone.

3. The first fishermen used bone to make spear prongs, hooks and needles for making nets.

Farming changes

The prehistoric farmers of Europe made small fields of any shape that was convenient. Not many animals were kept, so manure was in short supply. The Saxons introduced the ox-drawn plough into Britain in the fourth century. The fields then had to be made bigger because the oxen needed room to turn at the end of each line, or furrow.

Medieval farming

Seven hundred years ago, the farmland in Britain was worked by labourers known as serfs. The land around each village was divided into three huge fields. Each field had a different crop. One would grow wheat or rye, another barley, oats, peas, or beans, and the third was left without any crops so that it could recover. The next year, each crop would be grown in a different field. This was called 'crop rotation'.

A heavy plough was pulled by four to eight oxen. The coulter and ploughshare cut into the ground, and the mouldboard turned and buried the top layer along with its weeds.

Captabunt in animam iusti: + fan guinem innocentem condempnabut.

The medieval village was in the middle of the three fields. The serfs could take their pigs to graze on acorns in the woods.

Key words

Serf - a worker who was not allowed to leave the land on which he worked.

Fallow - land left unsown for a year.

The names remain

Many parts of our towns and cities have been built on land that was once used for farming. Sometimes the names of roads or places remind us of the past. A 'Drover's Lane' would have been a track along which animals were driven. Can you find any more examples in your own area?

Key

1. 1st field (Autumn-sown wheat or rye, harvested following summer)
2. 2nd field (Winter fallow, then spring-sown barley, oats, peas, or beans; harvested in summer)
3. 3rd field (Fallow for a year, may be used for grazing)
4. Manor House
5. Church
6. Tithe barn
7. Pound (stray animals kept here until they were claimed)
8. Woodland
9. Common land

Each serf had long strips of land in the three fields. The long strip was the best shape for ploughing with oxen and a heavy plough. Everyone planted the same crops at the same time and harvested the grain as a team. Beyond the fields were meadows for hay, and common land on which cattle could graze. The land was owned by the lord of the manor. The serfs paid rent for their land by giving grain or by working on the lord's own crops.

Britain was farmed in this way until about 1700. For many reasons it was not a very successful method of farming. A third of the land, the fallow field, could not be used. The hay meadows did not provide enough food for the livestock to eat over the winter, so many of the animals had to be killed. This resulted in a shortage of manure. Without manure, nutrients could not be put back into the soil.

The improving farmers

The open field system of farming carried on for hundreds of years. Then everything changed. The landlords were looking for new ways of farming which would be more successful. Keeping sheep was one way. The large open fields were divided up by walls and hedges into many smaller ones. By 1850, Britain was covered in a patchwork of small fields.

Jethro Tull

For thousands of years, seed had been sown by hand. In 1701, Jethro Tull, a gentleman farmer, musician, lawyer, and writer on farming matters, invented the seed drill. His horse-drawn drill carried the seed in large hoppers. The seed was fed down narrow tubes into a small furrow in the ground. Tull used parts of a church organ to make the drill. People laughed at his ideas, and his own farm workers went on strike. A hundred years later seed drilling was being used all over the country.

Seed sown by hand grew wherever it happened to fall. The seed drill sowed seed in rows. Tull made a horse-drawn hoe to clear any weeds from between the now straighter rows. This gave the turnips more room to grow and stopped the weeds taking nutrients out of the soil.

In some places you can still see traces of the strips farmed by medieval serfs.

Horses pulled the new seed drills. The horse harness was invented in the eighteenth century. From then on horses replaced oxen in the fields.

The turnip was a new food crop for animals. More animals meant more manure to replenish the soil.

The turnip arrives

Landlords started to grow new crops for feeding animals during the winter. One of these was the turnip. This was an important new crop. Animals could be put into the turnip fields to graze and their manure enriched the soil. Also, it was possible to weed between the turnips. One of the first landlord farmers to use this new crop was Viscount 'Turnip' Townshend. The Viscount grew wheat in one field, barley in another, grass and clover in the next, and in the last, turnips. The following year he grew the same crops but in different fields. This four-course crop rotation became a popular way of farming.

The use of the turnip meant that fields no longer had to lie fallow as they had in medieval times. Harvests were larger than ever. There was enough to feed the ever-growing population.

Viscount Townshend (1674-1738) was an English statesman. On his land in Norfolk he improved crop rotation and encouraged the growing of turnips.

New animals

The changes which happened in the eighteenth century turned farming into a new science. At the new agricultural shows, farmers met to see and discuss the changes that were being made. There were new machines for ploughing, seed-sowing and harvesting. There were also new animals to admire.

Changing the livestock

Sheep had been kept mainly for their wool. In the eighteenth century, there were more people to feed than ever before. Sheep now became important for their meat. The farmers wanted larger, heavier animals that provided more meat.

Robert Bakewell, a farmer from Leicestershire, introduced 'selective breeding'. With the open field system, everyone's livestock had grazed together. It was impossible to control their breeding. Now that the animals were kept in the smaller, enclosed fields, Bakewell was able to control which animals mated together. Only animals which had the right characteristics were allowed to mate. The young they produced also had these characteristics. With this selective breeding, Bakewell created from the old Lincoln Longwool sheep a fast-growing sheep with less wool and more meat. He called it the Leicester Longwool.

The Romney and the Lincoln Longwool sheep were once kept by medieval farmers. They were almost completely replaced by new breeds that produced more meat.

Robert Bakewell (1725-95) created the Leicester Longwool. He was famous for the gentle way he treated his animals.

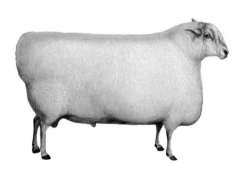

Robert Bakewell also bred Longhorn cattle. His new cattle produced very good beef, but not very much milk. The Colling brothers of Darlington used similar methods with Shorthorn cattle and produced animals that gave good milk and beef. Between 1801 and 1810, a bull known as 'The Durham Ox' was carried around the country on a special cart, because it was thought to be a perfect example of a Shorthorn bull. One of its ancestors had been a Darlington bull.

The Durham Ox

By 1800, farmers were raising cattle and sheep that were three times larger than they had been a hundred years before. They were also producing better quality pigs, poultry and horses. These methods are still used by animal breeders today.

Farmers from Britain, Europe and America came to agricultural shows each year to talk about the 'new farming'.

The harvest changes

Harvest time occurs at different times of the year, depending on where you live. It is the time when crops are gathered in, and for farmers it has always been one of the busiest and most important times of the year. In the UK, cereal crops are usually harvested from late July to September. Farmers with animals cut grass for silage in May and grass for hay in June and July.

From hand to machine

For centuries, farmers cut their cereal crops and grass with short, hand-held sickles. Later they used long-handled scythes. It was back-breaking work. This all changed with the invention of the reaping machine.

Patrick Bell, a Scottish man, invented the first reaping machine in 1826. It was horse-drawn and cut the crop with a scissor action. The crop was then gathered into bundles, or sheaves, and left to dry in the sun. Later reaping machines could also tie the crop into sheaves.

Key words

Silage - any crop cut when it is green and stored in an airtight container. It is kept for animal food.

Ricks - a large stack of hay, wheat or other crop.

Flail - a wooden pole with a short, heavy stick swinging from it.

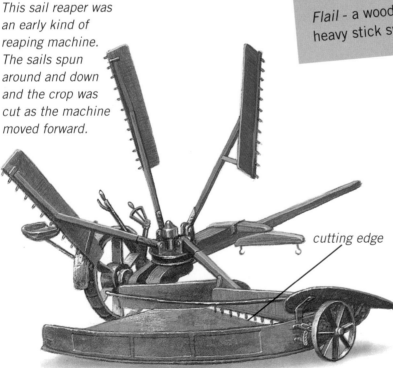

This sail reaper was an early kind of reaping machine. The sails spun around and down and the crop was cut as the machine moved forward.

cutting edge

When the hay and wheat were dry, they were put into a barn or built into ricks. The hay was fed to the livestock in the winter. The wheat or barley was threshed. It was beaten with hand-held flails. This loosened the grain from the rest of the plant. The grain was then thrown up into the air. The unwanted parts of the ear, the chaff, blew away and the grain fell to the floor. This was called winnowing.

Combine harvesters combine the jobs of reaping and threshing. The first combines were pulled by horses. Today, these large machines are powered by petrol or diesel engines. They can be used to harvest barley, wheat, oats, oil-seed rape and beans. The crop is stored in a tank and transferred to a trailer when the tank is full.

Today, both hay and straw (the wheat stalks left by the combine) are packed into brick-shaped or large, round bales in the fields by machines called balers. These are then taken to the farm and stored.

A steam threshing machine being driven by a steam engine. The man in the light-coloured jacket is forking the crop on to the machine. The rick, which is nearly all threshed, was raised above the ground, perhaps to keep it dry.

By 1850, steam engines had moved into the fields. They were used to drive threshing machines. Each machine could do the work of several men. The wheat was fed in at the top. It was threshed by several flails spinning on a drum, and the grain poured out the bottom. Most farmers did not need, or could not afford, their own machine. They hired the machines, and the men who used them. These teams travelled from one farm to another.

A modern combine harvester. The black horizontal bars at the front are the rotating blades. The driver sits in a dust-free cab.

The modern age of farming

In the last two hundred years farming has changed very quickly. More machinery on farms means less hard labour. Work is done much faster. More chemicals are used. The result is that fewer workers are required and bigger farms can be managed.

Following the changes

You may like to find out more about the farming changes that have taken place in your area. Visit local museums and libraries. Talk to older people, especially farmers, who may remember what farming was like a long time ago. In some farms there are still old farming tools and machines that you could draw or photograph.

The tractor

One of the most important machines on the modern farm is the tractor. It was invented in the USA in 1908 by Henry Ford. For a while it did not catch on in Britain, because the fields were too small and it needed room to turn. In 1935 Harry Ferguson invented a method by which ploughs and other machines could be fitted to the back of the tractor. They were powered by the tractor's engine and could be lifted for turning. This meant that tractors now needed less room. By the 1960s they had almost completely replaced horses. Today, tractors do a wide variety of jobs on the farm.

Harry Ferguson on one of his tractors. He has been ploughing. The plough is now raised so that he can drive away.

Tractors today can be fitted with attachments for many jobs. This one is pulling a forager. It is cutting rye grass which will be used to make silage.

Chemicals on the farm

During the years of the Second World War (1939-45) new chemicals were introduced to help farmers grow more food. These included insecticides which killed insect pests. New weed-killers and chemicals to deal with crop diseases were also developed. Chemical fertilizers meant that the farmer no longer needed manure to put goodness back into the soil. Farmers could now grow only crops if they wanted to. Chemicals also meant that farmers could grow the same crop year after year on the same piece of land. They did not have to rotate crops as before.

There are now fewer people working on British farms, yet they produce more food than they have ever done. Similar changes have taken place in other developed countries in Europe, in Canada, in the United States and in Australia. In the developing countries, the new machinery and chemicals have made less difference. In many parts of the world farmers still use methods that have not changed for thousands of years.

Dairy farming

There are a large number of farms in Britain which keep dairy cattle for milk. This milk is made into cream, butter, cheese and yoghurt. On one large, mixed farm in Warwickshire, England, ninety-five Friesian cows are kept for milking. On half of the land, good grass is grown to feed the cows. On the other half, cereals and root crops are produced.

The milking routine

The farmer and his farmhand take it in turns to milk the cows. They are milked twice a day, every day, at 5 am and 5 pm, until about two months before they give birth to their calves. In the summer, the cows have to be brought in from the fields. In the milking parlour, the cows stand on a platform. The farmhand cleans the cows' udders and then attaches the suction cups to their teats. A computer records how much milk each cow gives.

The parlour holds sixteen cows all together and each cow can be milked in four or five minutes. To milk the whole herd takes between one and a half and two hours. The milk flows into a huge tank where it is chilled and awaits collection by the milk tanker.

Friesian

Jersey

Guernsey

Milking facts
- A cow may spend eight hours a day chewing the cud (undigested grass).

- A dairy cow will produce between 16–20 litres of milk a day.

- In spring and summer, a cow will eat 70 kg of grass a day.

- Every herd has a 'queen' who usually takes the lead.

Friesian, Jersey and Guernsey cattle are kept for the milk they produce.

A year on the farm

From about mid-April to October, the cows live outdoors. When the ground starts to get muddy and wet they are brought inside. Each cow has its own cubicle bedded with straw. They eat silage. This is made from green grass, maize or kale which has been cut and pressed into airtight clamps. The yards and passageways between the cubicles fill up with liquid manure or slurry. Every day, the farmhand has to scrape this away with the tractor.

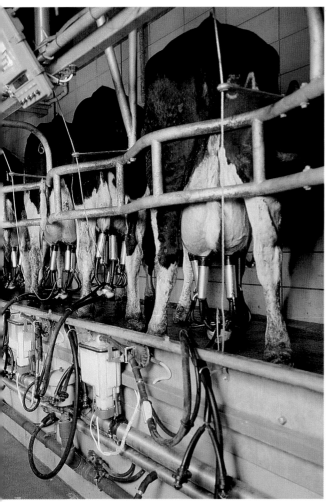

A modern milking parlour. The milk is passing through measuring bottles below the cows.

Hereford

The breeding cycle

A cow is usually two to two-and-a-half years old before it has its first calf. Cows will not begin to give milk until they have had a calf. On the farm in Warwickshire, the herd is an autumn-calving herd, which means that calving begins in September. The calves stay with their mothers for a few days, then they are taken away. Within a few weeks they are eating silage and hay. They remain inside until the following May. Some of the female calves will eventually join the milking herd. The rest are sold for beef. Adult cows must be pregnant again within three months of calving.

Charolais and Hereford cattle are kept to provide beef, rather than milk.

Growing vegetables

Many farmers grow vegetables as well as cereals and grass. On a small organic farm in Gloucestershire, grass is grown for a herd of sixty cows. Most of the work, however, involves growing wheat and vegetables such as potatoes, carrots, swedes, cabbages and leeks.

Farming without chemicals

This farm is farmed organically which means that artificial chemicals are not used on the land. Unlike other farms, chemical fertilizers cannot be used to make crops grow better. Instead, manure is used to put nutrients back into the soil. Crop diseases cannot be prevented by using fungicides, or weeds kept down with herbicides. Weeding has to be done by hand or machine. When the cattle become ill they cannot be given antibiotics. Cattle are fed organically-grown foodstuffs to keep their bodies free of chemicals. This kind of farming often means more hard work. Organic milk and vegetables are, however, sold at higher prices.

Cabbage planting. The planters put the cabbage seedlings on to rotating wheels. These plant the seedlings in neat rows.

These potatoes are dug up by the machine attached to the tractor and then collected by hand.

Key word
Drill - a machine used for making furrows, sowing and covering seed.

A year on the farm

The dairy cattle follow a similar cycle to those on a non-organic farm. Most of the cows have their calves between September and Christmas.

In between feeding and milking the cows, the farmer is busy with his vegetable crops. His diary would look like this.

OCTOBER

Carrot crop is ready. With tractor, pull machine through crop to loosen and lift carrots, shake away soil and leave them on the ground to be picked up. Sort and pack indoors between now and March.

Potatoes to be lifted with another tractor-pulled device. Pickers put them into buckets. Store for one or two months. Sort and pack as required from now until March.

NOVEMBER

Cut small, early cabbages as needed. Lift first of the leeks. Trim and pack other vegetables as required from now until February.

JANUARY

Manure spreading. (The cows spend every winter in an open cowshed. Last year's well-manured bedding straw is now spread on the fields. This manure is the organic farmer's only source of fertilizer.)

FEBRUARY

Lift rest of the leeks.

APRIL

Plant seed potatoes with mechanical planter. Plant carrot seed with drill. Prepare land for new crops.

JUNE

Leeks to be planted. Swede seed to be drilled. Plant young cabbage plants. (This is done by people sitting on the back of a tractor-drawn planter.) Start the weeding, by hand.

JULY

Potato leaves large enough to smother weeds. All other crops need weeding. Cabbage rows to weed with hoe pulled by tractor. (Weeding continues throughout August also.)

SEPTEMBER

Pull early carrots. Harvest wheat. Tractor-hoe cabbages and swedes. Calving about to start.

A farming diary

See if you can find out how vegetables are produced in your area - on large farms, smaller market gardens or even in people's kitchen gardens. Can you produce a diary that these vegetable growers could use to remind them of what they should be doing every month?

Sheep and other animals

Sheep are kept in most parts of Britain. They are particularly common in the colder, more hilly areas of the far north and west. This is because sheep are tough. They make good use of poor grass and need little attention. Sheep are kept both for their meat and their wool.

There are many different sheep breeds. Each has different qualities. Hill sheep are rough, tough and half wild. Downland breeds of sheep are not so tough. They were originally bred to live on the best grass and produce big, meaty lambs. Many modern farmers keep sheep which are a cross between these two.

Every summer, sheep are dipped in chemicals which kill parasites living on them.

Hill sheep give birth outside. Later, the flock is rounded up and some of the lambs are sold.

In hilly areas, lambing takes place in the spring, after the bad weather. In milder, lowland places, it may begin before Christmas. Many ewes (female sheep) give birth to twins or even triplets. Some ewe lambs may be kept to join the flock. The rest stay with their mothers until the summer. Then they are sold.

Pigs are also kept on British farms. On some farms, hundreds of pigs are kept in buildings where the temperature and food are carefully controlled. On other farms, tougher breeds of pigs are kept outside. Young pigs are fattened before being sold. Different-sized pigs are used to produce different kinds of meat. Bacon pigs are kept until they weigh 90 kilograms, heavy pigs used to make pies and sausages are kept until they weigh 110 kilograms.

Blue cross pigs are tough and are often kept outside in small herds on mixed farms.

Chickens are kept in large numbers to provide both eggs and meat. Egg-layers are often kept in battery houses. Each chicken is kept in a small cage. The eggs roll down into a tray and are then collected. Chickens and turkeys bred mainly for their meat are kept in deep litter houses. This is an open building. The birds can go into individual nesting boxes to lay their eggs.

All over Britain, farmers keep small numbers of chickens, turkeys, ducks and geese outdoors. At night they are locked into huts to protect them from predators such as foxes. Usually these birds only produce eggs and meat for the farmer's family.

Geese can usually roam free around farmyards.

Crops for sale

Commercial farmers grow crops for sale. Plantations are large farms that grow just one kind of crop. There are many plantations in parts of Asia, Africa, and South America. The crop is usually sold to developed countries such as the United States, Australia and countries in Europe.

In Malaysia, palm trees are grown on plantations. The oil from the palm is used to make margarine, cooking oil, soap, ice cream and animal feed.

Cocoa is grown by peasant farmers on small farms in West Africa. The white cocoa beans grow in orange pods on the trees. They are harvested, fermented in banana leaves and dried in the sun until they are brown. The beans are exported to Britain, France, the USA and the Netherlands. They are used to make chocolate.

Sugar cane is grown in most tropical and subtropical countries. The tall cane is cut and the sugary sap squeezed out. This is then boiled and processed into sugar.

A worker picking ripe coffee berries on a plantation in Tanzania.

Men harvesting sugar cane in Tanzania. They are using heavy, broad-bladed knives to cut the stems.

Coffee and tea are valuable cash crops grown on plantations. Coffee is grown in South America and East and West Africa. The bright red berries of the coffee bush are picked, dried and skinned to reveal the beans. Tea is grown in India, Sri Lanka and East Africa. The young leaves are usually picked by hand, then crushed and dried.

The world in your home
Study the food packets and labels in your kitchen at home. Where does the food come from? You may also like to visit a shop or supermarket. Make a list of the products and the countries they come from. Try to add as many countries as you can to your list.

A worker picking leaves on a tea plantation in Zimbabwe. She is throwing the leaves over her shoulder and into the basket.

Out on the ranch

Cattle are the world's most important farm animals. They are reared for meat, milk and muscle power. A third of the meat eaten in the world is beef. People in the developed countries eat the most beef. In other parts of the world, cattle are sometimes too valuable as milk producers or working animals to be eaten.

Farming on a little land

All over the world, cattle are raised on small farms. They graze on grass, but are also fed on hay, silage and concentrated foods. Sometimes the cattle are kept in small fields or enclosures, or indoors all the time. This is called intensive farming. The best beef and most of the world's milk is produced in this way.

On ranches, the cattle wander over huge distances and are rounded up by cowhands. This man is rounding up beef cattle in Nevada, USA.

These Friesian cattle live in a compound and are fed on hay.

The wide, open grasslands

In the Americas and Australia, cattle are also reared on huge, open stretches of land. They roam freely, eating only the grass that grows naturally. This is called extensive farming. This type of beef farming began in areas of natural grassland. In South and Central America, areas of the rain forest have been cut down and the land cleared to grow grass for grazing.

The rancher needs to round up the animals at certain times. For thousands of years, cowhands have been employed to do this in many different parts of the world. They round the animals up on horseback.

The beef produced on ranches is not considered such high quality as that produced by intensive farming. It is used to make hamburgers and processed meat products such as pies and tinned meat.

Counting sheep

Sheep are kept on farms all over the world. They are very important commercially in Australia, Europe and Argentina. The Merino breed is the biggest wool producer. In Australia, there are over 100 million sheep, most of them Merinos. They are often kept on huge areas of land and rounded up by people in all-terrain vehicles, such as jeeps, and on motorbikes. Once a year the sheep are sheared. The shearers remove the fleeces at a rate of 40-50 every hour. The sheep in Australia and New Zealand are also kept for their meat.

On the huge sheep farms of Australia, there may be 50,000 animals in a single flock.

The number of animals to the amount of land varies all over the world.

In Australia, where the grazing is poor, there are four animals to every square kilometre.

In the USA, and most of the world, the average is 25 animals to every square kilometre.

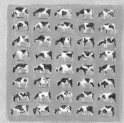

In the Netherlands there is intensive farming with 180 animals to every square kilometre.

Life on the prairies

Prairies are large areas of grassland, usually without any trees. In North America much of this land is now used to grow cereal crops. Vast areas of wheat stretch as far as the eye can see. This is the most impressive example of crops being grown for sale.

Prairie lands have warm summers and cool winters, and the right balance of rain and sun to grow crops successfully. Modern types of wheat produce a large amount of grain. Fifteen tonnes can be produced for every hectare of land. These crops use up 80 per cent of the soil's nutrients every year to help them grow. Because no animals are kept on the prairies, there is no manure to replace the goodness in the soil. Instead, fertilizers are used. Pests and diseases are controlled with chemicals.

Growing only one crop means that it is worthwhile for the farmer to buy large, expensive, specialized machinery. The high cost of the chemicals and machinery can be met by the value of the large quantities of grain.

The grain is stored under the right conditions in huge 'elevators'.

A fleet of combine harvesters cut the wheat on a prairie in Colorado, USA.

The grain is harvested by fleets of combines. It is stored in huge buildings. Ninety per cent of this grain is used to feed beef cattle and other animals raised on intensive farms. Vast amounts of grain are exported to other countries.

The USA and Canada are cereal-growing countries but they also grow other food. California, in the USA, grows grapefruit, peaches, apricots and grapes to make wine. Texas is famous for its peanuts. These are also grown in Alabama.

During the Dust Bowl disaster of the 1930s, many farmers in the USA were forced to abandon their homes and land.

The American Dust Bowl

In the 1930s, disaster struck the cereal-growing areas of West Kansas, Oklahoma, Texas, Colorado and New Mexico. Over-farming and droughts had turned the land into a desert. The wind blew the soil away, crops were smothered and houses buried. Nothing would grow and cattle died of starvation. During the severe drought of 1988, many farmers feared the same thing would happen again.

Field Facts

The world's largest field is in Alberta, Canada. It is used for growing wheat and covers 14,160 hectares. Into it would fit 283 average-sized British farms or 14,160 football pitches!

Farming for yourself

Subsistence farmers are farmers who manage to grow enough food for themselves and their families but cannot afford to grow enough to sell. Most subsistence farmers live in the developing countries of Asia, Africa and South America. They grow a range of cereals, fruits and vegetables. Many also keep sheep and goats for wool and milk. Cattle are kept mainly for farm work.

Precious rice

Rice is the basic diet for half of the human race. It is grown in China, India, Bangladesh, Japan and the countries of south-east Asia. In India, rice is the most important crop.

Rice seedlings are raised in nursery beds and planted out into the fields by hand.

Terraced paddy-fields in Nepal. The surrounding wall of each field prevents the soil being washed away. Terraces are a good way of stopping erosion.

Rice is grown in flooded paddy-fields. The water comes from the monsoon rains or from a flooded river. It is kept in the fields by low earth banks. The fields are ploughed with a simple wooden plough, pulled by a water buffalo or bullock. The rice seedlings are planted out into the fields in July. Four months later, the crop is cut with hand-held sickles. The crop is then threshed to loosen the grain and winnowed by hand to separate the husks.

This way of farming has been successful for a long time. But the population in these parts of the world is growing all the time. The soil is lacking in nutrients. Droughts, plagues and storms ruin crops and cause famine. Millions of people have died. In recent years, new methods and new crops have been introduced in some areas. These have helped some farmers. They are always looking for new ways to produce more.

This woman is winnowing. The wind blows away the unwanted chaff and the grain falls to the ground.

This croft is in Sutherland, Scotland. People have lived and worked on crofts since medieval times.

Living on a croft

Not all the farms in the developed countries are large profit-making businesses. Crofting is a kind of subsistence farming which takes place in the Highlands and islands of Scotland. The crofter rents between one and two hectares of land for growing mainly oats and potato crops. He or she may have four or five cattle and up to 100 sheep.

Crofts are not usually big enough to provide a living. Often the crofter will have other work such as fishing, running a shop or weaving. Many young people have left the crofts to work elsewhere. Others carry on the tradition. It is a hard and sometimes lonely way of life, but a beautiful place to live and work.

Growing fruit

A great variety of fruit is grown around the world. What grows where depends on the weather conditions, especially the amount of sunshine and water. Fruit grows on trees, vines, bushes and other plants. It is often grown on large plantations and sold to other countries.

The most nutritious part of the fruit crop is the fruit itself, or the seeds. Sometimes the leaves, stalks and roots are also eaten. Many people are needed to harvest a large fruit crop. This makes it an expensive luxury food.

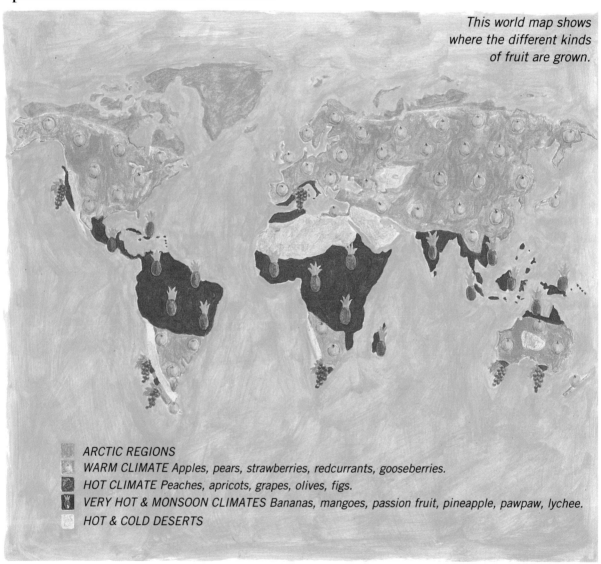

This world map shows where the different kinds of fruit are grown.

ARCTIC REGIONS
WARM CLIMATE Apples, pears, strawberries, redcurrants, gooseberries.
HOT CLIMATE Peaches, apricots, grapes, olives, figs.
VERY HOT & MONSOON CLIMATES Bananas, mangoes, passion fruit, pineapple, pawpaw, lychee.
HOT & COLD DESERTS

Fruit from Mexico

Mexico has many different weather conditions and soils. Farmers grow bananas on low ground in the rain forests and oranges on the sunny hillsides. They can also grow melons, strawberries and tomatoes in desert areas that have been irrigated. Most of these fruits are grown for sale in local markets, but some are transported to other countries. The farmers plan their growing so that there is fruit in the markets all year round.

Growing bananas

New banana plants are grown from roots that are taken from fully grown plants. The young plants need lots of water. If there isn't sufficient rain, water is channelled from nearby rivers. The plants have short roots and are easily blown over by high winds. Trees are planted between them to offer protection.

The plant's flowers grow at the end of a long stalk. This bends over and hangs down. The bananas grow from the flowers and point upwards, towards the sun. A bunch is made up of clusters called 'hands'. Each hand has between ten and eighteen bananas, but there can be between 100 and 200 bananas in each bunch.

The bunches of bananas are picked when they are still green. They are cut down with a large knife. When the plant has no fruit left it is cut down, but it will grow again in a few months.

Bananas that are sent to other countries are packed and stored in refrigerated holds on ships or aeroplanes. This stops them from ripening. At the other end of their journey they are stored in heating rooms. The temperature is carefully controlled. When they are just ripe enough, they are transported to the shops.

Bunches of bananas in a packing shed in Costa Rica. They are hanging on wires so that they do not get bruised by touching the ground.

In a Mexican market there is a wide variety of fruits, vegetables and other farm crops for sale.

Hothouse vegetables

In the USA and Europe large quantities of vegetables, such as peas and carrots, are grown to be frozen and sold in shops and supermarkets. They are frozen within hours of being harvested. Vegetables are grown in smaller amounts in market gardens. In southern Spain, large amounts of fruit and vegetables are grown in plastic greenhouses.

Spain has long, hot, dry summers. This is good for holiday-makers, but it makes the farmer's job more difficult. In the past, farmers grew only crops such as wheat, olives and vines that could survive in the heat with little water. Thanks to large-scale irrigation, southern Spain has been transformed. In the valleys behind the Plain of Valencia, the rivers are dammed in the winter and spring to prevent flooding. Water from reservoirs is carried to the fields in concrete channels. Thousands of small fields, called huertas, are now used to grow oranges, lemons, potatoes and rice.

In the Plain of Valencia, in southern Spain, irrigation channels take water to the fields.

Salad vegetables grown in greenhouses are picked by hand.

Water from deep wells has also made a great change in the Almeria province. The area around the town of El Eijido has been turned into a landscape of plastic. Plastic greenhouses cover an area of 12,000 hectares. Most of these greenhouses are owned by smallholder farmers. With plenty of water, they are able to grow large quantities of tomatoes, cucumbers, peppers, beans, cabbages, lettuce, melons and courgettes. The crops are carried by refrigerated lorries to supermarkets all over northern Europe.

Planting cabbage seedlings in a large greenhouse.

New crops

Better irrigation schemes may also help people in the developing countries to grow more food. In the future new varieties of vegetables may be grown. The winged bean could be one of them. Every part of it can be eaten. The Yeheb bush is able to grow in very dry places and produces seeds packed with nutrients.

Yeheb bush

Winged bean

Farming the waters

There is one place where people all over the world still find food by hunting and gathering: the sea. Fish are a good source of protein and in some countries a lot of fish is eaten. The richest fishing grounds are those just off the coast. Since the earliest times, fishermen have caught fish in coastal waters.

Modern fishing methods are very efficient. The fish are caught in huge nets. In many waters, overfishing is now a serious problem. Fish populations are falling. This has led to a renewed interest in fish farming.

On fish farms, fish are bred and raised just like cattle on land. Keeping fish in enclosed areas, specifically for food, has gone on from generation to generation in China. Carp feed on water plants and algae in the upper and middle layers of the pond. In the lower levels, dace feed on debris and material that drifts down from the top of the water. This keeps the water clean.

Dace

Salmon

Trout

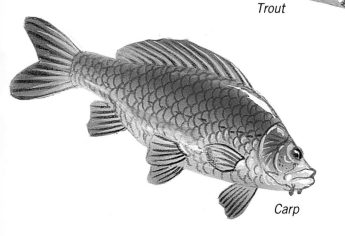

Carp

In other parts of the world, many of the traditional fish-ponds fell into disuse a long time ago. Salmon and trout farming, however, is now common in Europe and the United States. Trout are raised in ponds or fenced-off sections of rivers. Salmon are kept in large floating cages at the wide tidal mouths of rivers. A single farm may have as many as 500,000 fish at various ages. All their food is provided by the farmer.

A salmon farm in the United States. Fish farmers take care to keep their fish healthy. Diseases can spread easily when large numbers of fish are kept in small ponds.

Mussels

Oysters

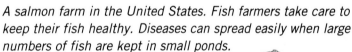

seaweed

In Japan, seaweed has always been an important food. It is grown on coastal seaweed farms. Seaweed provides a rich source of protein and in the future may become a more important food worldwide. There are other water-living plants that we may also be eating in the future. A blue-green algae forms a mat which floats on the surface of Lake Texcoco in Mexico and on small lakes in Africa. This is rich in protein too. Local people have been making it into biscuits for centuries.

In Ireland, fish farmers breed mussels on submerged ropes. In France there are oyster farms. The oysters are kept on raised platforms which are exposed when the tide goes out.

Beliefs and celebrations

Since the earliest times farmers have believed that storms, poor harvest and illness in animals are all aspects of nature which are controlled by gods or demons. They have believed that their farms will be safe if they perform certain ceremonies and pray to their gods.

Farming customs around the world

Each part of the farming year has its own custom attached to it. In most parts of the world, people celebrate the new year and a new growing cycle. In China, the new year is celebrated in the spring, before the new seeds are planted. People dance in the streets to scare away evil spirits that may harm the new crops. In Britain, maypole dancing celebrates the new life to come.

Maypole dancing in Britain is an ancient custom. The dancers celebrate the new, green life of spring after the long, cold winter.

Protecting the crops

People pray to their gods for help with growing the crops. The ancient Egyptians prayed to Khnum to bring the floods. The Mayas, Indians from Central America, made offerings of their own blood to the gods of the sun, wind and rain. In Britain, early scarecrows were just wooden crosses. They kept evil out of the fields. They were later dressed in clothes to confuse the devil. Animals were protected by horseshoes hung above doorways. They had to be nailed above the door with the prongs pointing upwards so that the luck would not pour out.

Some of the customs and beliefs of our farming ancestors, such as making scarecrows, continue today. Corn dollies (right) are made from the last stems of corn and were believed to contain the spirit of the corn.

Children taking part in the rice harvest festival on the Japanese island of Miyajima.

Celebrating the harvest

If the harvest is good, then people celebrate and give thanks. The Japanese celebrate the autumn rice crop. The spirits who protect the crop are thanked. There are processions, dancing and a feast of the newly-grown rice. In Kerala, India, the harvest festival is called Onam. Houses are decorated and the children weave flowers into mats. There are races in boats carved with snakes' heads and birds' tails. Native Americans traditionally celebrate the harvest with dancing and prayers. They dance to the gods who made the maize grow.

In the past, people also looked for ways of protecting the stored crops. They believed that a rick could be protected from fire by laying a pair of crossed scythes on top of it.

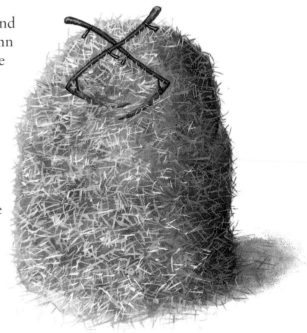

Chemicals on the land

Every year, the world's farmers produce more and more food. They do this by using more machines and more chemicals. They use herbicides to kill weeds and pesticides to kill insects that damage crops. Fertilizers are used to put nutrients back into the soil. Famers also protect their livestock from disease with antibiotics.

Many people are concerned about the effect that chemicals are having on the countryside and on our health. Chemicals can pollute the air, soil and water. Wild birds, animals and plants are killed by them. Chemicals given to animals may harm people who eat the meat.

Saving the birds

In 1939 a new pesticide called DDT was discovered. It was used to kill insects that caused disease and damaged crops. Later, people realized that it takes a long time to get rid of DDT. Birds that ate insects sprayed with DDT were getting a build-up of the chemical in their bodies. In the USA, bald eagles, brown pelicans, peregrine falcons and other birds were dying out because of the poisonous DDT. In 1972, the USA, Canada and other countries banned DDT. Since then, the populations of the birds have increased.

Crop sprays drift in the wind. They can harm people and animals, and kill wild plants.

Pesticide poisons pass along the food chain. Predators, such as owls, foxes or eagles are killed by them.

Natural enemies

Some farmers are controlling pests by introducing another animal which will eat them. In California, USA, the citrus crop is protected from the cottony cushion scale insect by a natural enemy, the vedalia beetle. In China, insects that attack the sugar cane are controlled by wasps at a third of the cost of using pesticides.

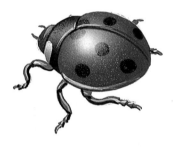

Ladybirds can be used to control pests such as scale insects which damage sugar cane crops.

Organic farming

In the USA and Europe, many farmers are changing to organic farming as a way of producing healthier food. This means that they do not use artificial chemicals. Instead compost and manure are used to fertilize the land and plants such as clover are grown to put nutrients back into the soil. Crops are also moved from year to year to starve pests of the crop they like to eat. Antibiotics are not used on cows. They are kept as healthy as possible by giving them the best organically grown foodstuffs.

Organic gardening

You might like to find out more about organic gardening. Can you find out about organic methods? Many gardening techniques used in the past were organic, because chemicals were not available. Older people may be able to tell you how they dealt with diseases and pests years ago.

Losing the land

Every year millions of tonnes of soil are blown or washed away from fields all over the world. This is called erosion. This is happening for many different reasons. In the developed countries it is often because the land has been overworked. In other parts of the world it is due to the loss of trees, overgrazing and droughts.

Blowing in the wind

In the USA, topsoil is being lost in some areas because it has been overworked. The same crops have been grown on it year after year with the help of chemical fertilizers. The soil is dry and exhausted. It is blowing away in the wind. This problem is now being tackled. In 1986, the Conservation Reserve Programme was launched. Many of the worst affected croplands have been turned into grasslands or woodlands. Topsoil erosion has been reduced by 610,000 million tonnes. Farmers are now finding other ways to produce more crops, for example, crop rotation.

The soil on this farmland in Rwanda is being washed away by the rain. Trees once held the soil in place by their roots, but they have been chopped down.

Taking control

In India, vast amounts of soil are being washed away by the rains. This is largely due to the clearing of forests. When mountain forests are cut down, there are no tree roots to hold back the soil or the water. This causes erosion and flooding. Very dry areas are turning into deserts.

The reasons for deforestation and desertification are very complex. Population growth, poverty, drought, and the loss of traditional farming methods are all at the root of the problem. People are often caught up in a chain of events that are not of their own making: the forests are cut down; firewood becomes scarce; people burn manure to cook with; less manure means fewer crops; animals graze on poor land; there is no regeneration and the soil erodes away.

Key words

Deforestation - the clearing of trees and forests.

Desertification - a process in which any grass or scrubland becomes more like a desert.

Regeneration - the process by which the forest plants are established again on land which has been cleared.

Erosion - the wearing away of the Earth's surface.

The Chipko Movement began in 1974 in the village of Reni in the foothills of the Himalayas. Local women hugged the trees of a nearby forest to stop government loggers chopping them down. This has inspired other communities to take the lead in managing their own environment, just as they used to in the past. In the state of Gujarat, many villages have planted forests on their grazing lands. The saplings are given to them by the forestry department, but the people have to protect them as they grow. The replanted trees are used for timber, fuel and animal fodder. More villages are joining the scheme every year.

The Chipko Movement in India began when the women of Reni stood in the way of the government foresters.

The future for farming

The human population is growing. In the future, the world will need more and more food. In Africa, South America and Asia, more is needed now, because many people are starving. Creating more farmland will destroy many natural habitats. Chemicals and machines are expensive and also damage the environment. Scientists are looking for other answers. Much of this work is being carried out in the world's laboratories.

With genetic engineering, a scientist can change a type of plant without having to first breed thousands of unsuitable ones.

Improving crops and animals

Scientists are trying to improve some of the more common crops such as millet and sorghum, which is a grass similar to sugar cane. Much of this research is being carried out in the developing countries. They are studying the genetic codes of crops and animals. Genetic codes control the characteristics of a living thing. Biotechnology is the new science of changing these characteristics to make new crops. It is hoped that these new crops will not be affected by disease, pests and drought and will produce huge harvests.

Scientists are trying to improve animals, such as deer and camels, which live well on poor grazing land. They are also working on changing the genetic make-up of animals to make them breed younger and quicker and produce more offspring.

This wheat has a disease called ear blight. It is diseases like this that scientists are trying to stop.

Many people are concerned about these new laboratory methods. They believe that putting genetically altered plants and animals into the wild is dangerous.

There are many other schemes for producing more food. Land is being reclaimed from the sea. Deserts are being irrigated. Greenhouses are used to grow crops out of season. Other ideas involve going back to old methods, such as crop rotation, where different crops are grown in a regular order to avoid exhausting the soil, or simply by improving what already exists.

The Earth's future is also our own. Farmers need to find new ways of producing more food, but without harming the environment. Everyone should have enough to eat and a world worth living in.

Index

Published by BBC Educational Publishing,
BBC White City, 201 Wood Lane,
London W12 7TS

First published 1994
© Andrew Charman/BBC Education 1994
The moral rights of the author have been asserted.

Paperback ISBN 0 563 355417
Hardback ISBN 0 563 355425

Colour reproduction and cover origination by Goodfellow & Egan, Cambridge
Printed and bound by BPC, Frome, Somerset

Photo credits
Beamish, The North of England Open Air Museum, County Durham **pp. 16/17**; BBC /Luke Finn **pp. 2, 37 (top)**; BBC/John Jefford **p. 3**; British Library **p. 10** *Add MS 42, 130 f.170*; Cambridge University Collection of Air Photographs **p. 12**; Environmental Picture Library **pp. 28, 46 (top)**; Eye Ubiquitous **p. 41**; Robert Harding Picture Library **p. 35 (top)**; Grant Heilman Photography Inc **pp. 5 (top), 28/29, 30, 30/31, 39**; Holkham Hall **p. 15 (bottom)**; Holt Studios International **pp. 4, 17 (bottom), 19, 20/21, 22, 24, 26 (top), 32 (top), 35 (bottom), 36, 37 (bottom), 42, 46 (bottom), 47**; Hulton Deutsch Collection **p. 18**; Hutchison Library **pp. 44/45**; Lawes Agricultural Trust, Rothamsted Experimental Station **p. 15 (top)**; Leicestershire Museums, Arts and Records Service **p. 14 (right)**; Panos Pictures **pp. 5 (bottom), 26 (bottom), 27, 32 (bottom), 33 (top)**; Range Pictures Ltd **p. 31**; University of Reading, Rural History Centre **pp. 13, 14 (left)**; The Scottish Highland Photo Library **p. 33 (bottom)**.

Front cover: Holt Studios International **(main picture)** wheat field; BBC/Luke Finn **(bottom right)** loaf of bread.

Illustrations
© Andrew Wheatcroft (pages 6, 7, 8, 9 and 45) © Mike Atkinson (pages 7, 9, 14, 20, 21, 24/25, 29, 31, 33, 37, 38, 39 and 43) © Roger Stewart (pages 10/11, 12/13, 16, 40 and 41) © Rachel Ross (pages 23, 29, 34 and 43).